A special thank-you for

_____

You are special to me.
Thank you for being my mom.

With love and gratitude,

_____

Date

_____

the thank you series™

*O*ur purpose at Howard Publishing is to:
- *Increase faith* in the hearts of growing Christians
- *Inspire holiness* in the lives of believers
- *Instill hope* in the hearts of struggling people everywhere

Because He's coming again!

Thank You Mom © 2003 by Howard Publishing Company
All rights reserved. Printed in the United States of America

Published by Howard Publishing Co., Inc.
3117 North 7th Street, West Monroe, Louisiana 71291-2227

03 04 05 06 07 08 09 10 11 12   10 9 8 7 6 5 4 3

Stories by G. A. Myers
Edited by Between the Lines
Interior design by LinDee Loveland and Stephanie Denney

ISBN: 1-58229-275-2

thank you
mom

a collection of poems,
prayers, stories, quotes, and
scriptures to say thank you

HOWARD
PUBLISHING CO.

thank you

When people tell me, "You're just like your mother," I have the perfect comeback: "Thank you!"

thank **you**

mom

Dear Mom,

Thank you! Thank you for your sheltering warmth when cold winds of adversity blew against my heart. Thank you for your tears of empathy and joy. Thanks for looking beyond my flaws and seeing my promise, for holding on to the warm, fuzzy treasures of my past while mercifully forgetting my cold, prickly failings. Thanks for always wanting the best for me, bringing out the best in me, and believing the best of me.

You are a fortress of courage and strength. You're selfless, nurturing, and good. You encourage your family, cheering on those you love with enthusiasm and passion.

Your influence and spirit will live in the hearts of those who love you. I don't say it enough, can't express it adequately, but I hope you know how much I love you.

Thank you, Mom.

Love,

Job
10:12

CEV

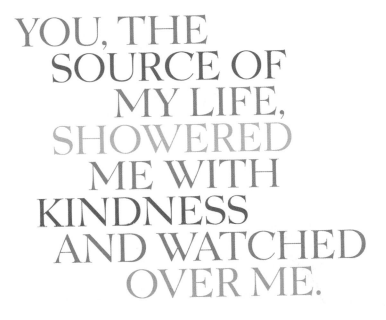

YOU, THE
SOURCE OF
MY LIFE,
SHOWERED
ME WITH
KINDNESS
AND WATCHED
OVER ME.

Ah, then how sweetly closed those
    crowded days!
The minutes parting one by one like rays,
That fade upon a summer's eve.
But O, what charm or magic numbers
Can give me back the gentle slumbers
Those weary, happy days did leave?
When by my bed I saw my mother kneel,
And with her blessing took her nightly
    kiss;
Whatever Time destroys, he cannot this;
E'en now that nameless kiss I feel.

—Washington Allston

Award-Winning Mom

Sam listened intently and nodded knowingly as the dean of the prestigious business college glowingly described Andrea Jefferson, who was about to receive an honorary doctorate. To everyone at the celebration, Andrea was the consummate professional: always dressed in a business suit, her shiny black hair pulled back tightly against her head. Everything about Andrea communicated propriety, self-control, and accomplishment.

That's why Sam wore a Cheshire cat smile. He knew a different Andrea. As Sam watched the woman on the platform sitting starched, straight, and sophisticated, his mind wandered to another remarkable day twelve years ago when Andrea had distinguished herself in a different way.

It was a cool fall day at the private school where Sam was in sixth grade. He was bright, well-liked, and ambitious, and with all of his heart he wanted to play football for St. Augustine's. But Sam was one of the shortest boys in his class and didn't have the stocky build coaches looked for in a player. Nonetheless, his mother, Andrea, believed in his high energy and determination and encouraged Sam to try out for the team. To everyone's amazement, he made it! The coach saw the same fire in Sam and liked his enthusiastic support of the team.

When game time came around, however, the coach shied away from putting Sam in the game. He was afraid Sam wouldn't be able to hold his own against other, much larger opponents and would get hurt.

Sam's lack of playing time didn't dampen Andrea's enthusiasm. Every game, rain or shine, she sat in the stands—starched, straight, and sophisticated. While other parents showed up in jeans and tennis shoes, Andrea came directly from the office, wearing a business suit, high-heeled shoes, and her uncompromising hair style.

Some players might have been embarrassed at having such an out-of-the-ordinary mother, but Sam loved being able to spot her easily among the crowd. Every time he came out with the team from the locker room, he would wave at her enthusiastically and cross his fingers in a display of hope that *this* time he would get to play.

The team performed well throughout the season, and the final regular game would determine whether they qualified for the district championship. Sam still hadn't played. The first half of the game was close. With every touchdown, St. Augustine's would gain, lose, then regain the lead; and the crowd in the packed stadium would shout their approval and encouragement. All except Andrea, who sat interested but composed.

At halftime the score was tied at twenty-one. As the teams left the field for the locker rooms and some second-half strategy, Sam passed the area where Andrea was seated. She clapped politely, and Sam's answering smile showed off a deep dimple in his right cheek. But she could see in his eyes that he had accepted that he probably would never get to play. This was his last chance, and too much was at stake for the coach to put in someone unproven.

The coach followed the rest of the team, and Andrea managed

to catch his attention. Feeling bad about not letting Sam play all season, the coach approached to explain things to the boy's mother.

"You know, Mrs. Jefferson, I admire your son a great deal. He supports the whole team, and his spirit really helps drive us. I wish I could play him, but he's so small I'm afraid he'll get hurt out there."

Andrea smiled gently at the coach and said, "I appreciate your wanting to protect Sam, coach—I really do. And I understand your not playing him, especially in such a tight spot. But I do want to say that I believe a boy's physical stamina is often in direct proportion to the strength of his spirit. Don't be afraid, coach. I'm not."

Her quiet but powerful words echoed in the coach's mind as he continued to the locker room.

The second half of the game was even more heated than the first—a battle of wills that brought the spectators to their feet every few minutes. As the fourth quarter wound down, the score was tied again.

Neither team had been able to score on their recent possessions. With three minutes to go, the coach needed to break the gridlock. He needed something the other team didn't expect—a secret weapon—someone quick but small enough not to draw the opponents' attention. He looked over at the bench and scanned for just the right player. There sat Sam, faithfully cheering on his teammates. It was risky to put Sam in at this point. He showed up at every practice and worked hard, but he'd never been in a real game. *Don't be afraid...* The coach heard Andrea's words again.

With less than two minutes left on the game clock, the opposing team had the ball. "Sam!" the coach called out. "You're in for Daniels at defensive right end."

Sam was so shocked he didn't respond at first. But his teammates nudged him, and he ran out onto the field, fastening his helmet.

When Andrea saw her son join the lineup, her stoic expression began to dissolve. As Sam looked up into the stands and raised his crossed fingers, she stood and raised her crossed fingers in return.

In the next two plays, the opposing team advanced to within twenty-five yards of the goal. One minute and twenty-five seconds remained in the game. The next play was a screen pass around the right end—right through Sam's position. The ball was hiked, the quarterback went back, and the screen started to form. It looked good. They had fooled everyone—except Sam.

Sam got down low and, at the eight-yard line, right in front of where Andrea was seated, snaked his way through two huge blockers and lunged to make the tackle. His helmet knocked the ball loose, but it also stunned Sam. Players struggled to get the ball as fractions of seconds seemed to pass in slow motion. Andrea leaped to her feet and ran down the bleachers toward the field, waving her arms and yelling, "Go, Sam, go!"

Sam recovered and snatched the ball. He had never been ruled down, so as the crowd screamed, Sam ran toward the faraway goal line. A lineman flew between him and a would-be tackler. Sam stole a quick glance toward the sidelines and couldn't believe what he saw. There was his mother, running down the sidelines in pace with him!

Large portions of hair hung down, shaken from the pins that held each strand in place, and he could barely hear her over the crowd. "Run, Sam, RUN!" Her suit jacket had been thrown to the ground, and the hem of her blouse escaped the waistband of her dress slacks and flapped freely as she ran as fast as she could, gasping for air. Looking uncharacteristically undignified, she shouted her encouragement without reserve. "Only thirty-five more yards to go, Sam. Keep running! You're going to make it."

Andrea had abandoned her shoes back at the bleachers, and her nylons were now in shreds, but she didn't notice. "Go, Sam, GO!" she screamed at the top of her lungs.

Finally, and with one great lunge, Sam dove over the goal line. As the referee raised his hands to signal a touchdown, Andrea ran onto the field, jumping and yelling in celebration of her son's victory. She wove her way through the players to Sam and gave him a huge hug, tears of pride streaming down her cheeks. The two embraced in celebration until they realized they had caught the stares of players and fans alike.

Mother and son looked at each other and realized how silly they must look but they were too excited to care. They simply shrugged and joined the team in their jubilation. As Sam's teammates lifted him onto their shoulders, the coach extended a hand to Andrea. "Well," he said with a grin, "I'm glad you weren't afraid. Now I'm not either." With that, he turned to Sam. "Looks like you'll be a starter next year!"

"Andrea Jefferson!" the voice came over the loudspeaker, snapping Sam back to the present.

But the image of one disheveled and never-more-beautiful Andrea was permanently etched in his memory. Now as the refined Andrea rose to receive her award, Sam walked to the stage. He took his mother's arm in his and raised crossed fingers with the other hand. "I'll keep my shoes on if you don't mind," he said with a proud smile, "but I'd like to walk beside the woman who has run beside me all of my life." Andrea's eyes filled with tears of love as Sam whispered, "Go, Mom, go."

thank you

God doesn't allow

us to choose our

mothers. This is

good. Otherwise

everyone would

choose you.

a blessing
for you

$\mathcal{M}$ay the Lord bless you, Mom, for all that you do,

$\mathcal{F}$or the years you've spent caring for me.

$\mathcal{Y}$ou've given me life and helped me to grow,

$\mathcal{M}$aking me all I can be.

mom

mom

May your selfless outpouring of tender devotion

Be replenished with blessings unleashed.

May your goodness and virtue be the crown that you wear,

Reflecting God's glory and peace.

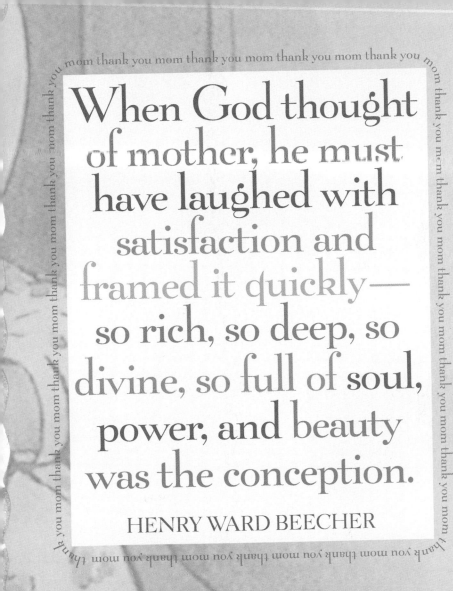

When God thought of mother, he must have laughed with satisfaction and framed it quickly— so rich, so deep, so divine, so full of soul, power, and beauty was the conception.

HENRY WARD BEECHER

thank you

When I catch myself

doing something that

reminds me of you,

I thank God for my

connection with such

a wonderful woman

—and I smile.

A mother is the truest friend we have, when trials, heavy and sudden, fall upon us; when adversity takes the place of prosperity; when friends who rejoice with us in our sunshine, desert us when troubles thicken around us, still will she cling to us, and endeavor by her kind precepts and counsels to dissipate the clouds of darkness, and cause peace to return to our hearts.

— *Washington Irving*

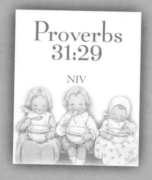

Proverbs
31:29

NIV

MANY
WOMEN
DO NOBLE
THINGS,
BUT YOU
SURPASS
THEM ALL.

Exercise in Love

Cheryl looked in the mirror one more time as though what she saw might change with a fresh glance. It didn't. Ten extra pounds had shown up on the scales over the last month, and there was no hiding it. "Where did it all come from?" she whispered to herself. But she already knew the answer.

Randy, her boyfriend of nearly two years, had told her exactly one month ago that he wanted to break up now that they were attending separate colleges. They had talked of marriage just the previous summer, so the news shocked Cheryl and hurt her deeply. Depressed and far from home, Cheryl comforted herself with food.

Now the spring semester was over, and she was going home for a visit before returning for summer session. But instead of excitement, she felt dread at having to face everyone. She slumped onto the bed among the piles of clothes and cried yet more tears from her seemingly endless supply.

Her mother knocked at the door a half-hour later, right on time. Cheryl had never known her mother to be late for anything. Diane was an ambitious worker and, since her husband's death in a small plane crash, a single mother with four children to raise. She was tall and slender, an attractive woman with wavy, dark brown hair and sparkling blue eyes.

Cheryl mirrored her mother's features right down to the contagious, slightly tilted smile. Aside from their ages, the only difference between them now, Cheryl noted with dismay, was her extra weight.

The minute Diane entered the room, she could tell something was wrong. But she decided to let Cheryl fill her in when she was ready and simply gave her daughter a warm hug and told her how much she had been missed. "We're going to have two wonderful weeks together," she said confidently. "Now, let's get you home."

Home was the most wonderful word Cheryl could have heard at that moment. Home was a shelter where she felt safe and loved;

her mom had always made sure of that. And Cheryl had always admired her mother's wisdom and intuition. She seemed to sense what her kids needed even before they knew it themselves.

On the ride home, Diane did most of the talking, bringing Cheryl up to date on all the hometown news. About thirty miles from home, almost before she knew what she was doing, Cheryl blurted out, "Randy broke up with me, Mom."

Diane hid that she had already figured this out and responded sympathetically. "I'm sorry, baby. I know how hurt you must be." Then she parked along the side of the road, gave her daughter a long hug, and listened to the tearful account.

"How will I ever get over it, Mom? I feel so sad I don't think I can stand it," Cheryl said between sobs.

"You may never get over it, honey. You don't really get over the loss of someone you love. But you'll see—the pain will lessen, and little by little you'll get back to enjoying your life."

Cheryl nodded and then, eager to move on to more pleasant topics, asked, "What's new with you, Mom?"

"Well," she said, "I've started walking every morning before I go to work, but it's tough to stay motivated. While you're home, will you help me keep it up?"

It felt good to think about someone other than herself for a change, and Cheryl responded eagerly. "Sure, I can do that. But Mom, you're already on your feet all day at work!"

Diane chuckled. "Yes, but it's not the same thing as working up a good sweat and getting in shape."

"Well, you can count on me," Cheryl assured her, amazed as usual at her mother's energy.

"Great! And, you know, I've been wanting to try out some new little restaurants at lunch. Why don't we meet downtown at noon? Then, on my days off, we can visit some museums and art galleries. Your brothers and sister never want to go with me, but I'd like to have a little more culture than video games and sports in my life," Diane said laughingly.

"Wow, Mom, you're really expanding your horizons, aren't you?" Cheryl laughed, her mood improving.

For the next two weeks, Cheryl got up early and bounded into her mother's room each morning, eager to accompany her on her daily walks. At lunch they sought out-of-the-way tearooms or bistros, where they tried various gourmet salads and fruit dishes. Cheryl had never known her mother to take time out for lunch, and she felt especially privileged to have this time with her.

Exercise in Love

In the evenings and in their spare time, they always found something fun to do—another museum to visit or a fun trail to take at a local nature reserve. As they hiked through the town or through the forest, Diane walked enthusiastically and listened intently, ignoring her aching feet and weariness from work.

Finally it was time for Cheryl to return to school. Diane gave her an especially big hug as they parted. "I've never had a more delightful two weeks!"

"Me either!" Cheryl agreed, hating to see her mother leave after bringing her back to campus. She waved until the family car was out of sight.

Cheryl spent the next couple of days getting back into the routine at school. On the third morning, she was stunned as she caught a glimpse of herself in a full-length mirror. She had been so active at home that she lost all of the weight she had gained!

She quickly dialed her mother's number and started the conversation with an investigative question: "Mom, have you been walking since I left?"

"No, I have so much to do in the morning that I haven't had time. I have to get the kids going and make my lunch for the day..."

"So you're not still going out for lunch?"

"Oh, no, it's too busy to get away," Diane answered nonchalantly. "Is everything OK, sweetie—do you need anything special?"

Cheryl looked in the mirror once more, her suspicion confirmed. Once again, her mother had known exactly what she needed and filled the need without her even realizing what she was doing. Her mother had known that more than losing the weight, Cheryl needed to feel loved and to focus on something positive. She had found a way to help her daughter feel better about herself *and* about her physical condition. Asking for Cheryl's help was just her way of lovingly and subtly helping *her.*

"No, Mom," she answered with a smile. "I already have something special—you! Thanks for a terrific spring break. What in the world would I do without you?"

"Well, don't worry, baby. I'm always here when you need me."

"I know, Mom," Cheryl said affectionately as a tear came to her eye. "I know."

Exercise in Love

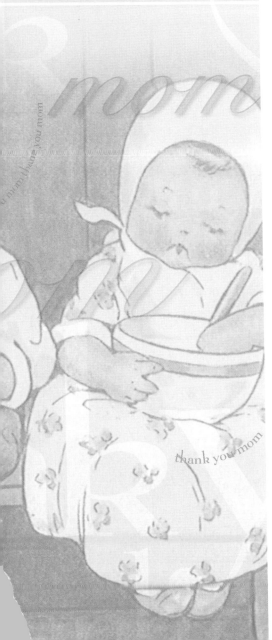

thank you

Cookies and
carpools were the
daily brush strokes
of beauty and
meaning as you
painted love on the
canvas of my heart.

Youth fades;
love droops;
the leaves of
friendship fall.
A mother's
secret love
outlives them all.

OLIVER WENDELL HOLMES

Thank you, God,

For pretending not to notice that one of

Your angels is missing and for guiding
    her to me.

You must have known how much I
    would need her, so

You turned your head for a minute and
    allowed her to slip away to me.

Sometimes I wonder what special
    name you had for her.

I call her "Mother."

—*Bernice Maddux*

thank you

Thank you for

making me feel

ready to conquer

anything...and for

watching over me

until I really could.

thank you

mom

Dear Heavenly Father,

When You created Mom, You must have known how richly she would bless the lives of others. She's graceful and kind, and her patience runs deep as the ocean. She knows and gives what her family needs. She gives her time and her heart to help and heal those in need.

Bless her with long life and purposeful, happy days. May she feel loved and respected, not for what she does but for who she is. As she has brought warmth and tenderness to her family, please enfold her with that same comfort and assurance.

Walk faithfully by her side as she has walked faithfully with me. Cheer, encourage, and comfort her, as she has been Your hand extending these blessings to others. Open the floodgates of heaven and pour upon Mom the blessings she lavishes on those she loves. Thank You for my mom. Thank You for the enduring, precious legacy her life and love have given me.

Amen.

There is no love
on earth, I think,
as potent
and enduring
as a mother's love
for her child.

ANN KIEMEL ANDERSON